Simple Science for Homeschooling High School

Because Teaching Science isn't Rocket Science!

Lee Binz,
The HomeScholar

First Printing, 2015

Printed in the United States of America

ISBN: 1517740762
ISBN-978-1517740764

Simple Science for Homeschooling High School

Because Teaching Science
isn't Rocket Science!

What are
Coffee Break Books?

Simple Science for Homeschooling High School is part of The HomeScholar's Coffee Break Book series.

Designed especially for parents who don't want to spend hours and hours reading a 400-page book on homeschooling high school, each book combines Lee's practical and friendly approach with detailed, but easy-to-digest information, perfect to read over a cup of coffee at your favorite coffee shop!

Never overwhelming, always accessible and manageable, each book in the series will give parents the tools they need to tackle the tasks of homeschooling high school, one warm sip at a time.

Everything about these Coffee Break Books is designed to suggest simplicity, ease and comfort - from the size (fits in a purse), to the font and paragraph length (easy on the eyes), to the price (the same as a Starbucks Venti Triple Caramel Macchiato). Unlike a fancy coffee drink, however, these books are guilt-free pleasures you will want to enjoy again and again!

Table of Contents

Introduction

You Can Teach Science!

I want to help you have more fun with science in your homeschool high school. The good news is it can be simple for you AND fun for the kids. Your child may even get more college admission offers and bigger scholarships because of your homeschool science classes.

Homeschoolers ask me many questions about teaching science. Before homeschooling my own kids and becoming The HomeScholar, I worked as a registered nurse. I loved being a nurse and I loved biology and chemistry when I was in college. I was a homeschool mom who loved science, but I know not everybody feels the same way.

Although I do love biology and chemistry, I've never taken a physics class in my entire life. I still managed to help my children become successful in science. One of my children earned bachelor's degrees in electrical engineering and computer engineering and his masters in computer science, and is now working at a high tech company!

Some parents love science like me, but I'm fully aware there are parents who hate science. (That's how I felt about teaching physics.) You can teach science the easy way or the hard way. If you love science, you may actually enjoy the hard way!

Some parents get truly excited about teaching science, technology, engineering, and math. They could do science in their sleep and with both hands tied behind their back. If you don't love it, and even fear it, try teaching science the easy way instead. You can also choose to teach science inside the box (in the traditional way) or outside the box.

Whether science is your passion or the bane of your existence, let me show you how you can make science simple in your homeschool. You can encourage the love of learning and help your children enjoy science! Teaching your children to love science could help them think of the subject fondly and prepare them for college and career.

Encouraging the love of learning will help them learn even more and they will be able to enter college with the love of learning intact. With a college-prep education in science, your child will be ready to tackle any challenge in the future while enjoying the love of learning today.

Chapter 1

Five Reasons to Teach High School Science

Parents sometimes look to me to reassure them it's OK not to teach science in high school. The bad news for them is, it really is important! The good news is, I will show you how to make it as painless and enjoyable as possible in the pages to follow!

When pressed, I give five strong reasons to face the situation and teach science.

Reason 1: Science is required for high school graduation

Almost all school districts require science as part of their core curriculum. It's a core element of graduation in many states. When you look up your state requirements, make sure they are your state homeschool requirements because they may be different from state public school requirements.

Reason 2: Science is also required for college admission

Colleges usually demand more than what is required for high school graduation. In general, as part of a college prep education, colleges look for at least three years of science with at least one lab. If you plan to teach four years of science, that's great, you can exceed expectations. Your child can earn better scholarships by taking science every year.

Four years of high school science can be important, even for kids who have absolutely no inclination of a science-related career. It's a good idea to include a full four years of science. It can pay off in the long run. Besides, teenagers change their minds and may someday decide on a science-intensive career. You want them to be ready!

Reason 3: High school science helps students build critical thinking skills

Learning critical thinking through science prepares children for the ACT test and understanding science helps them better analyze data and form accurate conclusions. As adults, they will be able to think critically about news reports or studies in the paper. The thinking skills learned in high school are skills used daily. Science helps form these critical thinking skills.

For children who love science, it is equally important to study English, art, and the liberal arts. It helps them develop critical thinking skills in a different way. They need a college prep education in order to pull all the pieces together. People who make great scientific discoveries also have information beyond science they can bring to the forefront. They can take their acquired knowledge about the human body and other information about engineering and come up with amazing new prosthetic devices.

Reason 4: Science demonstrates that students have the ability to work hard

Colleges and employers both want people with a strong work ethic. Strong, academic subjects on your child's transcript show they have the ability to work hard. Four years of science shows that your child worked hard for four years. Your child can be successful getting into college and career because they have demonstrated their hard work.

Reason 5: Science is required for STEM careers and colleges are willing to pay for it

STEM stands for science, technology, engineering, and math. The good news is, if your child has an aptitude in these subjects and you're preparing your child for a STEM career, they are eligible for some fabulous scholarships. Keep an eye on the big picture; you're investing money in science and math curriculum for good scholarships in the future.

If possible, graduate your child with a calculus and a physics class if they are looking forward to a STEM career. This isn't always possible and it's not mandatory (you can search for a college that doesn't require these subjects instead). There are some great jobs available for those with STEM degrees.

Teaching vs. Facilitating

You do have to cover science in your homeschool, but that doesn't mean you have to "teach" science. Instead, you can facilitate science. Once your children are high school age, your job will change and you'll become the facilitator or project-manager. You're the one who makes sure they learn and not the one who has to teach the entire curriculum.

What does teaching science look like at home? When I was homeschooling high school, my children would read the textbook with the teacher's manual in their hands. They would work through each lesson on their own; if they were stuck, they would look at the solution manual and compare the answers to their own work. They would teach themselves through the questions and answers given in the curriculum.

When it was time for a test, I would take away the solution manual and give them the test. Because I was not perfectly prepared to teach, being a good facilitator and not a good teacher, I didn't know what the answers had to look like, especially in physics. When marking tests, I made sure the answers looked exactly like those in the solution manual. It didn't matter if my children claimed their answer meant the same thing – each answer had to be exactly the same as the answer key, unless they could prove they were correct.

My best friend's children had learning challenges. All through high school until her children were 18 years old, she read the science textbook aloud to her then 18-year-old sons to help them learn. Then they chatted together about the answers in the solution manual.

Your goal is to encourage your children to start becoming independent learners. I wanted my children to do all of the reading themselves since they were capable. My children completed all of the experiments with an adult standing-by. It was a little different with biology because I love it so much and I tried to teach them how fun and exciting it was. Unfortunately, of all the sciences, they liked biology the least.

The bottom line is that science is a core subject students need to cover in high school. If your child wants to go into a scientific or medical profession, then biology, chemistry, and physics are critical.

Many universities offer scholarships when children are well prepared in science, technology, engineering, and math. In addition to preparing them for graduation, college admission, and career requirements, teaching science can lessen overall college expenses through scholarships!

Chapter 2

Avoiding Common Mistakes

You certainly want to prevent chemical explosions or failed attempts at proving physics principles in your science classes. However, there are more common, less spectacular mistakes that are easy to avoid.

Common Errors When Teaching Science

1. Physics failure

Physics failure happens when you focus so much on moving your child through science that you introduce a science before they have the math required for it. Physics requires advanced math (pre-calculus). Don't allow your child to attempt physics before advanced math is completed. This will cause a physics failure.

Parents often teach children physics and are surprised when their children fail. Often it's because they haven't looked into the prerequisites required for success. If you have a non-math child, skipping math-based physics may be something to consider. Some public schools offer botany and ecology classes and they might fit the bill perfectly in your homeschool. General science, earth science, and physical science are other options.

2. Science avoidance

Science-haters who don't prioritize the subject, often avoid it. Purchase a curriculum to guide you and keep you on track. Be consistent.

Struggling learners will be more successful if you can separate their learning challenge from the subject as much as possible. For example, if your child has severe dyslexia, you can read to them and carefully assist them in following directions for each lab, step-by-step. If your child has dysgraphia and trouble writing, you can ask for oral presentations or computerized reports instead. If your child struggles in math, you can avoid excessive math, or work on the math orally instead of avoiding physics altogether.

It's important to do what works for your family. Some parents may want to judge and accuse you of spoon-feeding your child, but you need to do what works for your child. Others may not understand your child's unique learning challenges.

3. Not prioritizing your weakness

If science is your weakest link, you need to prioritize it to get it done. In general, you should cover your weakest subject first. Science is the first subject you cover each day. Make it your priority. Don't let one day go by without doing science. Cover the weakest link first and leave the fun stuff for last.

Science doesn't have to be the very first thing your children work on once they drag themselves out of bed. Make it the first conscious subject they do - after breakfast and after your first cup of coffee, but definitely before noon. I put off art; we went months without art in our homeschool. You can't put off science for long – you need to prioritize it.

Make science a priority financially as well. Buy your science curriculum first. Science curriculum can be expensive; the textbooks tend to be a bit pricey. Science equipment can also be expensive. Don't put off buying a science curriculum. I know what homeschooling is like; you would rather buy curriculum for every subject other than your weakest.

Re-purchase science curriculum if necessary. If you start the year using Bob Jones' science but you find you can't stand it or your child hates it, you need to buy a new curriculum. Make sure you can teach your weakest area in the simplest and easiest way possible.

4. Cobbling together curriculum

Don't piece a science curriculum together. If science is your weakest subject, don't go the eclectic route because of the risk that you simply won't get around to it. You won't pull it all together, you won't get the resources you need, and it won't happen.

I encourage you to buy a packaged curriculum instead. Let a homeschool curriculum hold your hand so you can be consistent. Otherwise, it's easy to let it slide. The next thing you know, you're behind in science and don't know how to dig your way out.

5. Going too fast

On the other hand, science may be your greatest strength. If so, fight the urge to accelerate too quickly. You don't have to cover eight sciences – only three sciences are generally required. It would be great if your child exceeds expectations, but don't accelerate so quickly that your child has outpaced their math-level.

If science is your greatest strength, you can find college-level lectures once you get past the high school curriculum. There are also community college classes you can take once they get beyond the point of using high school curriculum. When you enroll your children in community college, keep in mind that it can be a rated-R environment. Some of the challenges we experienced in community college came up in science classes.

If science is your strength, your children may be excited about science. Ensure you give them a good base line science education so they can go into a career in science. Cover the core classes of biology, chemistry, and physics.

6. Not keeping pace in math

Sometimes math can be a stumbling block. Your child may be so excited about science they forget to finish math. If science is your greatest strength, emphasize math as well. Cover one level of math per year. Your goal is to have your child learn pre-calculus or calculus by the end of high school.

It's common for a child to end up with many credits in one high school subject. If a child's strength is music and they attend a public high school, they may end up taking choir, band, and orchestra every single year. At the end of four years, this child will have earned 12 music credits. Your science-loving child can also earn multiple science credits per year. If your child is learning science on their own, you can capture any delight directed learning and award high school credits.

Chapter 3

Which Science Should You Teach?

When deciding which science to teach, first check your state law for any homeschool (not public school), science requirements. Requirements vary by state. Check out the article on my website, "Know Your State Homeschool Law" for help finding the requirements in your area.

Once you've checked out your state law, look into possible colleges. Requirements vary from college to college. Look at colleges and programs your child might be interested in and make sure you cover the science prerequisites they will need to gain admission.

Most colleges want to see at least one of the core sciences, usually biology or chemistry. Only children who are going into STEM careers, or a science-based college, need biology, chemistry, AND physics. Make sure your child takes three credits of science, including one with lab. Some colleges require more and some colleges will suggest specific sciences, such as biology or chemistry.

Homeschoolers often think there is an 11th commandment, "Thou shalt teach biology, chemistry, and physics." I'm here to tell you that you don't have to teach all three sciences. Not all children get into (or should get into) physics because it requires so much math. You can easily branch out and choose to teach other options, such as astronomy, geology, or botany.

To cover your bases, I suggest teaching your child biology, and then adding chemistry if possible. Chemistry only requires Algebra 1 level math; it is completely different from biology so usually if a child doesn't like one science, they'll like the other. Cover at least one or more sciences beyond the core biology and chemistry classes. Ensure at least one class includes lab. Labs help your child learn more because of the hands-on work they entail. They will also help prepare your child for college and college sciences.

Core Sciences

Biology, chemistry, and physics are the core sciences. Each time you cover one of them, you have the option to go back and cover the next level of the subject. You can start with "Biology 1" for instance, and then teach advanced biology and call it, "Biology 2." Your child could also take "Advanced Chemistry" after the first year of chemistry, and "Advanced Physics" after first year physics. You don't need to teach in that order, though. There are only four years of high school and you only need to teach three science classes. Not every child will take all six. Usually, students choose only one of the advanced sciences if interested in a STEM career.

Physical science and general science are optional; they are not prerequisites for biology. I suggest starting with biology in ninth grade for a more impressive college prep education demonstrated on your child's transcript.

Once you've covered at least one of the core sciences, you can start considering sciences outside the box. This can help not only non-science kids, but also those planning careers in science. Ensure that any science-related delight directed learning your child is engaging in also goes on your child's transcript. It is a way to exceed expectations in the sciences so your child can earn bigger scholarships.

Science Options Outside the Box

You don't have to stick to the core sciences. Astronomy is a great option. Anyone can go outside and stargaze. All you have to do is get a telescope and it's a lab science. You can use the workbook that comes with the telescope.

Botany and ecology are sciences often taught in public high schools. Many public schools require ecology in ninth grade. There are hands-on lab materials available. Check out the Home Science Tools website for great options. They offer water-testing kits to test your local rivers, ponds, streams, and oceans to study their ecologies.

The history of science is another possibility. It's a great option for history loving kids and can help convince them that science is cool. Your child's history credits should remain separate from a history of science credit. Colleges want to see four credits of history, including American history, economics, and government.

There are great curriculum choices available for the history of science. Instead of a curriculum, you can use a timeline to look for scientists and read biographies on each of the scientists.

Marine biology is a common science taught in my state since we are near the ocean. Marine biology can be fun. You can also choose to teach microbiology, which is the science of studying tiny critters (microorganisms) using a microscope. The lab could be expensive since you need a microscope, but you can teach microbiology all the way through college level.

If you choose to think even further outside the box, you can teach the science of anything. One homeschooler I know chose to study the science of mushrooms (mycology) every year of high school. Another homeschooler loved birds and studied birds. He wrote about birds and it was published in a bird book. He included ornithology (the science of birds) on his transcript every year.

Another option is to look at the activities your child is involved in for delight directed science ideas. For instance, if your child is involved in civil air patrol, they may enjoy learning about aeronautics. One of the high schools in Seattle specializes in aeronautics, so it's not as unusual a class as you might think.

Here are more choices, depending on your child's interests:

- Equine science for the child who works with horses or is a vet assistant
- Geology for the rock collector
- Herpetology for the child who loves to keep reptiles and amphibians as pets
- Horticulture for your master gardener
- Meteorology for your storm chaser
- Ornithology for the child who loves birds
- Zoology for your animal lover
- Robotics for the child who enjoys Lego Mindstorms or is involved in First Lego League

I personally took zoology in college and loved it; this science was helpful in my career as a nurse because many things I learned were applicable to my job.

If your child is in Boy Scouts, Girl Guides, or a similar organization at which kids work on badges, check out the work they do to earn those badges. Your child may have enough science related badges to create a class around them. Each scout badge is like a unit study. Collect all the unit studies together until you have enough hours to create a high school credit.

Another popular activity is robotics, the First Lego League, or Mindstorms. If your child loves robotics, you need to cover biology and chemistry. You also need to ensure your child completes a level of math each year. I know how much time it takes. Children can love it so much they can spend all their time on it and neglect math and other sciences. Kids involved in robotics are more likely to go into a science career, so make sure you include core science and core math in your plan.

Research science is yet another possible class. I know there are some kids who love to spend time in a lab looking through a microscope, doing research or studying DNA.

Any competitions your child is involved in can count as science credit. This includes science fairs or the Science Olympiad. Your child's papers or projects completed for a science scholarship also count.

Keep in mind that in public schools, electives are often chosen according to the teacher's interests. But you're not a public school. You can choose electives based on your child's interests. Don't feel shy about adding any outside of the box subjects to your transcript.

For more reading on science outside the box, check out my article, "Would a Nature Study Count As a Lab Science?" on The HomeScholar website. If your child is ready for college level classes, go to the Coursera.org or MIT OpenCourseWare websites.

For more information on delight directed learning information, check out my articles, "Maximize the Fun Factor" and "Delight Directed Learning" at www.TheHomeScholar.com.

Computer Science

Another outside of the box science option is computer science. To consider it a science class instead of a technology class, it usually needs to include programming or coding. Computer science is a perfect delight directed learning class; many kids love it.

Computer literacy is an extremely valuable skill. College campuses love kids with computer experience. Computer literacy can help your child get a great job on campus. It can give them a competitive advantage for college and career. Give your child credit for the work they've done.

You can also create a class using a programming curriculum. If you want to put it together yourself, then you might want to look at www.Code.org. It's an excellent online resource. My computer scientist son recommends it. If your child isn't sure they will like coding, then all you have to do is click on the start button on the website and try an hour of coding with your child. Children as young as eight can enjoy coding with cartoon characters, but there are tutorials for high school as well. This can be a way to get beginners interested in coding. There are also some beginner classes available at the Khan Academy website.

If your child is already computer literate, you can give them credit based on the skills they possess. If it's simple computer literacy, then I would consider it a technology credit instead of a science credit. But if your child is even more computer savvy - programming and using computer languages - then listing it as a science credit makes sense. You may be able to talk to your teenager and ask what computer languages they know to give you the words you need.

Let your children engage in delight directed learning and choose what they want to work on themselves. Make sure you as the parent record what they work on and for how many hours on the transcript and course description. You might be surprised how easy it is for your children to exceed expectations in science if they cover core sciences and coding.

The computer science skills my son learned were so valuable on his college campus that he (and his friends) got part-time work at the computer technical help desk. It paid better than a minimum wage job, so those computer science skills paid off; they helped him pay some of his college expenses.

For more on teaching computer science in your homeschool, check out my article, "Teaching Geeks" on The HomeScholar website.

Chapter 4

How to Teach Science

How do you teach science to make it interesting? Biology, chemistry, and physics are all so different that it's possible for a child to love one, and absolutely loathe the other two. You may not get to the point where they love all three core sciences – that is unlikely. Do your best, get your child's feedback, and be consistent, but you may not get them to love the science you're working on. Move on to the next science the following year and you may find they like it.

It can be shocking to think about how much you did not learn in high school. You may have the desire to learn science alongside your student. Many homeschool parents enjoy this for specific subjects because they get a do-over for their own public school education. It's not for everyone though (and it was not for me).

Homeschool curriculum has improved immensely since I homeschooled my own children. There are many online and digital resources available; there's no shame in using them.

Seven Tips for Teaching Science

1. Use a homeschool curriculum with answer key

Pulling subject matter together using a variety of resources can work for many parents, but if you feel insecure, I strongly encourage you to use a regular homeschool curriculum with an answer key instead. The answer key will be your best friend. You don't need to know anything about the subject; it will tell you the answers every time.

2. Enlist the help of groups, tutors, co-ops, and online classes for support

Purchase video supplements. Look for extra videos on chemistry or biology at Khan Academy to help supplement your science class. You can also collaborate with another homeschool family and teach science together; this method was popular when I was homeschooling and even before then. It doesn't require a co-op; you only need to find a homeschool friend who likes science.

I often see two families share the load. For example, an art-loving mom and a science-loving mom might join forces, with one teaching science and the other teaching art.

You can also create groups to enjoy experiments together. This can be helpful especially with mixed abilities, such as learning challenges and giftedness. In a group, kids can all work together with the microscope or telescope. Any challenges or quirks may not be evident as they work hands-on together as a group and have fun.

If you're stuck, you can enlist tutors or join a co-op. A homeschool co-op is often a good place to find a tutor. The person who teaches chemistry at your local homeschool co-op may be willing to come to your home and tutor your child. If your child has learning struggles, a co-op may not be the best bet; their learning challenges can be visible by everyone and it can cause your child to doubt themselves and their abilities.

3. Encourage multi-level learning

Kids don't have to be the same age to learn together. All of your children can learn biology at the same time. Your high schooler can learn at the high school level, while your middle schooler works through the book that came with the microscope, and you pick up your younger child to show them what's being worked on. Multi-age learning can be fun, especially in science. Science doesn't have to have a grade level attached to it. You can teach many sciences to different age groups and difficulty levels at the same time.

4. Study at a steady pace and finish one level a year

Don't put off science if it's yours or your child's weakest subject. Put science first every day and get it done.

5. Master the vocabulary

The best way to master any subject is to master the vocabulary. Research shows that vocabulary is critical for academic success. As your child memorizes words and their definitions, they learn new ideas.

Vocabulary itself represents 80% of comprehension of a new subject. The number one way to ensure your child is more successful in college is to teach them to master the vocabulary first. If your child studies economics and takes the time to master the vocabulary, they will be more successful at learning the subject.

One way to cover vocabulary is to review unfamiliar words each morning. I did this with my kids as part of our morning meeting each day. There are free vocabulary resources available. Donna Young's website has many vocabulary resources that can help your child master science vocabulary easily.

As long as you review words each morning, you'll be surprised at how much your children know by the end of each week, simply through repetition. Vocabulary is a skill your children will take with them. Whether in college classes, or on-the-job training, learning the vocabulary is key to getting ahead. Children and adults alike will be successful when they've learned the vocabulary, as it makes up 80% of what they need to know.

6. Have a morning meeting

In high school, you become less a teacher and more your child's project manager. The job of a project manager is to check in on a daily basis to ensure the work is done. You, as the homeschool parent, can do a quick check-in with your child every day.

Set a goal to hold a morning meeting five days a week. If you only get to it one or more times, consider it better than none at all. A morning meeting only takes fifteen minutes per child at the most at high school level, even if you check in with all the child's subjects.

Discuss your expectations for the day. For science, review vocabulary words, what today's lab experiment entails, or discuss the previous lesson and their last lab experiment. Whatever you do during your morning meeting, remember that your role has changed. Spending 15 minutes with your child checking-in each morning can be part of a successful high school experience. You are acting as the project manager who facilitates learning and does not lecture. For more on morning meetings, check out the article on my website, "Have a Morning Meeting."

7. Start with biology

Independent learning is a process. The ability to work independently in biology seems to come early in the process. Learning biology on their own is a good way for kids to take on some responsibility. I've seen children learn biology successfully, all on their own; it can help them feel more confident about learning other subjects independently. They can be responsible for reading chapters and working through assignments on their own, as my children did. They did everything on their own and I merely held morning check-ins and corrected tests.

The Road to Independent Learning

I am happy to share how my children learned to work independently in science. But keep in mind that every child and family is unique.

We used Apologia Biology in our homeschool. I made a list of assignments that told my children what pages to read or what lab or test to complete. I prepared it in advance during the summer months. It was in checklist format, so I could easily see if tasks were checked off and completed each day.

Our morning meeting included biology. During that meeting, I went over their vocabulary words, and would sometimes (though not often) ask them questions found in the textbook. Then they were responsible for reading each chapter on their own.

The labs were a little different. I'm a nurse, and I love biology. I loved every dissection and every microscopy lab. Sometimes I had trouble giving the microscope to my children to use, but I don't believe I taught them anything. I was merely present in the room when they did their experiments.

For biology labs, kids are either working with expensive microscope equipment or are wielding sharp dissection tools; not wanting them to get hurt, I was always in the room. They read the labs on their own and followed the directions. I watched, usually while folding laundry.

Once the experiment was complete, I left them alone to complete lab write-ups. I asked for a paragraph from each of them, explaining what they did and learned, as well as a drawing, graph or chart. At the end of the day, I looked at their lab report to make sure they had written a paragraph (not just a sentence) and had included a chart or drawing. If both were present and I understood the purpose of the experiment and its result, then I gave them 100%.

When it was time for a test, I simply handed them the test, confiscated the solution manual, and walked away. I corrected the tests while they began working on their next subject. I gave them a grade, wrote it on a piece of notebook paper I kept in each of their binders, and then had them correct any wrong answers.

My children were beginning to learn independently. They did all the reading and I didn't lecture (except about how expensive the microscope was).

I know other successful homeschool mothers who take a much more hands-on approach. Dealing with learning challenges, they read the entire chapter, or carefully assist their children in following directions for labs. It's important to remember to do what works for YOUR family.

I became less involved each year of high school. I found that chemistry didn't require as much help, so we didn't include it in our morning meeting. The labs were rarely dangerous, so I would just peek in sometimes. I felt completely overwhelmed and didn't understand the physics. They worked completely independently on physics!

Learning to become independent is a process that has to start somewhere. You will know what your own child is capable of doing!

Chapter 5

Including Science Labs

Colleges usually want to see at least one high school science that includes a lab. Facilitating a lab science usually means ensuring your children don't stab each other in biology, blow anything up in chemistry, or fall off a ladder in physics. I'm sure you're up to the task.

What is a Science Lab?

There is no nationally recognized definition of a high school science lab. The U.S. House of Representatives' committee on science and technology formed a sub-committee on research and science education, which conducted research and issued a report on high school lab science. It concluded there is no recognized definition of "high school lab science." The report says there is no commonly agreed upon definition of high school laboratories among researchers or educators. High school labs can be hands-on, virtual, or video-based.

You have a lot of flexibility when it comes to science labs. Most colleges don't mention including a lab every year. The College Board's national recommendations don't include science every year. They do state that science teaches students to think analytically and apply theories to reality. Prepare your children for what they're going to face in the work world and at a university. Get to know colleges and learn what they want from your child, but don't panic about labs.

How to Teach a Science Lab

Making sure your kids don't get hurt is easy for a homeschool mom. It's what you have been doing since they were young. Teaching a science lab is right in your wheelhouse.

How do you include labs at the high school level, without signing up for courses outside the home? You CAN teach a lab at home. The materials are easy to access; I recommend checking out Home Science Tools. Much homeschool curriculum also includes a package of all the materials you need: all the chemicals for chemistry, all the critters to dissect, or all the equipment you need for biology. Open the box and start working on the science lab at home. Science labs can be fun to share. Your child can work with siblings, or with a friend you invite to join you in the comfort of your own home.

When your child takes a course outside the home, it can be as uncomfortable as being in a public school. If your child has a learning challenge, it could be awkward to sit next to a child without a learning challenge. A profoundly gifted child could make others feels stupid when they work together. It's not necessary to take a lab outside of the home.

When you teach your homeschool science lab, you can choose only hands-on experiments. You can dissect critters if you want. If video labs work best in your homeschool, you can choose video-based experiments instead. It's your choice.

When you teach a science lab, keep your expectations simple. Provide loose supervision to make sure nobody gets hurt. Do your best to complete the experiments that are part of your curriculum. If you're using a science curriculum and have completed 75-80% of the suggested experiments, then you can consider your lab done.

If you're piecing things together (you're an eclectic homeschooler who loves unit studies and delight directed learning), I encourage you to organize one experiment per week. Delight directed learning labs might include attending robotics club once a week, or working with the vet once a week.

Whether your child is working on virtual, hands-on, outdoor, or indoor experiments, lab reports can demonstrate that your child has done the work required to call it a lab. I sometimes gave my children grades based on how annoyed I was with their performance. If their lab reports didn't annoy me, I would give them 100% because they had done a good job and completed what was required. Sometimes I gave my children 90% because I was slightly annoyed; they either didn't provide enough detail or forgot to include something.

I gave them even less if I was annoyed. Once, my son Kevin completed a lab write-up on white paper using yellow pencil and I couldn't read it at all. I was annoyed and gave him a terrible grade. It isn't unreasonable to give a grade based on annoyance if you remember that public schools will often award a grade for merely turning in the lab report.

Most colleges do not require a documented science lab. In case your child wants to attend one that does, it can help to keep your lab reports in case they ask for a written lab report. Colleges will sometimes offer the option of taking the science portion of the ACT test, the ACT Subject Test, or the AP exam to meet the science requirement.

Writing lab reports can prepare your children for college labs. My children had to write a lab report every time they had a lab class. They expected it; they weren't freaked out at all and were well prepared. This was not because we had done everything perfectly in our science labs, but because we were consistent.

For more information on teaching a lab, check out the article on The HomeScholar website, "You CAN Teach High School Science Labs."

Chapter 6

Choosing a Science Curriculum

There are many options available, but choosing your curriculum is more about how well it fits your child than anything else. It's like shoe shopping; no matter how cute the shoes are, if they don't fit, they're not going to work. The same is true for curriculum. No matter how shiny and new the textbook, no matter how highly reviewed the curriculum, and no matter how much you love the author, it isn't going to work if it doesn't fit your child.

Four Tips for Choosing a Science Curriculum

1. Use a homeschool curriculum

My most helpful tip for choosing a curriculum is to select a self-teaching curriculum designed specifically for homeschoolers. A public school chemistry curriculum would assume you already know the subject and have been teaching chemistry for years. When you use a homeschool curriculum, it assumes you know nothing about the subject.

You want your high schoolers to learn to teach themselves. Most textbooks are designed to teach children something they don't already know. Kids can learn on their own, and moms do not have to learn everything about the subject for the children to be successful. I didn't have a clue about physics and I was barely able to keep up with chemistry. Yet, my children excelled in science in both high school and college.

2. Get your child's input

Make sure the curriculum is meaningful to your child. If possible, have them look at the book or video and see if they like it. However, every time I showed my own children a textbook or an online video before I bought a curriculum, they couldn't have cared less. If that's your child's attitude too, make sure they know they have to do what you choose. Seek your student's feedback first though, because some kids can have strong opinions.

3. Use your child's math level as a guide

Keep in mind that biology does not require any specific math expertise. Chemistry requires a good understanding of Algebra 1. Don't start physics until your child has completed Pre-Calculus, because it's math-based. You want your child to love science, not to be distracted by the math involved or feeling in over their head.

4. Stick to tried and true curriculum

As you look through curriculum options, try to find a tried and true curriculum; it's usually your best option. New curriculum comes out every year, but until you've read reviews and talked to people who have used it, you won't know how it's going to turn out (even if it's from a successful publisher). The latest and greatest curriculum may also be untested and unproven. The tried and true has been used successfully by many different homeschoolers. The best preparation for college requires an easy to understand, successful curriculum.

Keep in mind that books change when new editions and updates are released. Each time a new edition comes out, you need to do your research and find out if the new version can be as successful as the old one was. Sometimes a new edition is written by a completely different author, so look over each one carefully.

Curriculum Suggestions

I don't usually recommend specific curriculum because I know it's more about fit than the curriculum itself. However, I do recommend Jay Wile's publications because my children used them with great success. He writes from a Christian perspective, but I still recommend his books for homeschoolers who are not Christian because the science is so strong and they are thorough textbooks. He is the author of *Exploring Creation with Biology*, *Discovering Design with Chemistry*, and *Exploring Creation with Physics*. I know Jay Wile personally and his books provide excellent college preparation.

My sons got A's in college physics after using Jay Wile's books in high school. My son, Kevin, referred to his high school physics and chemistry books while he was in college. Those science textbooks were some of my best buys when I was homeschooling because my children used them for five years.

Science Curriculum Options

Here are more science curriculum ideas:

- Ecology – Check out *Ecology: A Pocket Guide* and do a search for free ecology lesson plans online.
- Astronomy – If your child loves stargazing, check out *Signs & Seasons: Understanding the Elements of Classical Astronomy*. Purchase a great telescope and PRESTO! It's a lab science! You can also check out the college level lecture series called "Understanding the Universe: An Introduction to Astronomy" by The Great Courses.
- Marine Biology – Check out my "Ideas for Marine Biology" post on TheHomeScholar blog for some great resources.
- Computer science – Check out languages such as C++ or Java. The Code Academy website offers comprehensive and free online lessons.
- Geology – Check out *Creation Geology: A Study Guide to*

Fossils, Formations, and the Flood. I also love resources from NorthwestRockAndFossil.com.

Your science lab might include rock hounding in your state. The book, *Modern Rock Hounding and Prospecting Handbook* will help you get started.

- You may also want to check out Novare Science & Math.

- For more homeschool curriculum science options, check out the index of Cathy Duffy's science reviews on her website.

- If you're looking for even more great science options, check out the curriculum and materials available at Home Training Tools. You'll find most of what you need there – microscopes, telescopes, lab materials, textbooks and supplements. Ask questions and they will point you in the right direction and help you find the best-rated, tried and true curriculum.

Do you have to use a science curriculum in order to teach high school science?

No. Many homeschoolers pull together their own resources, use unit studies, or use outside the box resources.

One of my friends used a high school textbook from the local dollar store for science. She used the table of contents as her outline. Then she looked for hands-on experiments to teach the concepts in to her children in a more interesting way. She used it as a jumping off point so she would know what to cover in order to call it a physics class.

Chapter 7

How to Save Money on Science

When you invest in science, you improve your child's chances of earning college admission and scholarships. Invest your money in science resources, and your teen will have more career opportunities now and as an adult.

I can't believe how well teenagers with science experience are paid as technical assistants in a lab, working as assistants in an IT department, or doing coding. The technical assistants at my children's college earned $35 per hour, sitting at desks studying and waiting for students to come to them with computer technical problems. Investing in science can also mean a higher income potential for your child in the long run.

The cost of science class is what concerns parents, though. It is best to have a lab for all of your science classes in high school, but keep in mind that only one science lab is required. Remember that biology is the most expensive, because a microscope is involved along with all the critters to be dissected.

In the real world, people can't always afford the entire curriculum, including the lab equipment. If you're tight on money and simply can't spend another cent, then skip the biology lab, or try to borrow or share equipment with another homeschooler. There are chemicals and hardware necessary for chemistry class, but it is less expensive than biology.

Of course, one way to save money is to avoid teaching science! I do not recommend this! Instead, use a tried and true curriculum. When a curriculum that has been effective for ten years releases a new edition, the old edition may be available for \$5 on Amazon instead of \$50 for the brand new version. Use the tried and true curriculum since it's usually less expensive.

Contrary to what people might tell you, tutors and expensive online classes are not necessary. Buy a tried and true curriculum. Use library resources. Videos are a great science-teaching tool. Pick up some lined notebook paper for lab reports. Saving money means doing it yourself.

Chapter 8

Science Record Keeping

You need to keep records of high school academics, of course. Keep science tests, quizzes, and lab reports. You will also want to keep any written papers. Keep a list of resources used, such as textbooks and fields trips. When you use a textbook, it's helpful to take a photo of the cover and table of contents. These will help you create course descriptions easily. Keep what your state law requires along with anything colleges may ask for. One college asked us for a lab report, so I was glad I kept my children's hand-written reports.

Keeping all of this information – tests, quizzes, lab reports, and lists – was extremely helpful. When I created each course description, I was able to write a long, detailed description of what my children did. I used the table of contents in my descriptive paragraph, and listed each test, quiz, and lab report.

How to Calculate Science Grades

When grading assignments, it's easiest to make a quick estimate of your child's grade.

- Give your child 100% or an A if you're not annoyed and they did what you asked, or if your child loves the subject and gave it their all while producing high quality work.
- Give your child a 90% or a B if you are slightly annoyed and you know they could have done better and wish they had given more effort.
- Give them a grade of 80% or a C if you are terribly annoyed, but they kept advancing toward the next level.

This method also works when you give grades on a transcript. If you haven't

kept any records at all, the transcript is due tomorrow, and you have to give a grade on the transcript for Biology 1, ask yourself:
- Were you annoyed?
- How annoyed were you?
- Did your child love the subject and do good work?

This makes grading much simpler. Check out my "Quick Grading Estimate" on my blog at:
www.TheHomeScholar.com/blog /grading-estimate

When your child takes an honors class, the topic of weighting grades often comes up. I do not recommend weighting grades. Every public school has different ways of weighting grades and each state has different ways of weighting grades.

For example, if your child receives a perfect grade in an honors biology class in California, they are awarded an A, which is equal to a 5.0. In Illinois, a 4.5 awarded in an accelerated class becomes a 5.0 in an honors class. If you're in a

New Jersey public school, you are awarded 4.67 if it's college prep, 5.0 if it's honors, and 5.33 for a perfect score in an AP class. In South Carolina, the numbers are even stranger: college prep biology is awarded 4.875, honors 5.375, and an AP or community college class 5.875.

This frustrates colleges. They receive transcripts from all over the country and all grades are weighted differently. The first thing colleges have to do is un-weight the grades so students can be compared fairly. That's why I don't recommend weighting grades.

You are the school and you get to decide whether you weight grades or not. If you are going to weight grades, here is how you can make it easier. If your child took an honors class, you know your child has done more than high school level, and could add 1.0 to the grade. Instead of a 4.0, they would get a 5.0.

Another way to weight grades is to add to the credit value. If your class is a one-credit honors class, you could consider it a two-credit class. Whatever grade they earn weights twice as much. You would then calculate their GPA based on the weighted grade, which would likely improve their GPA score. I'm only giving this example for people who feel as if they need to weight their grades. Check out the article on my website, "Why I Do Not Recommend Weighting Grades" for more information.

Class Titles

Each science class needs a class title on the transcript. The title can be taken from the subject on the textbook. If the book is called *Exploring Creation with Biology*, the name of the class can be "Biology." You can add the words "with lab" if you included a lab, i.e., "Biology with Lab". Your class title is not the name of the textbook, so don't name it, "Exploring Creation with Chemistry." Use the name of the course subject.

Sometimes it can be helpful to use an acronym in your class title if your child has taken any classes in science outside the home. It's extremely helpful if your child took the CLEP to call it "CLEP Biology." If your child took a class at the local community college, for example, Highline Community College, you could call the class "HCC Biology 101 – Introduction to Biology."

On the transcript, the grade should include your child's daily work as well as tests, reading assignments, lab reports, and quizzes.

Credit Hours

It's easy to determine credit if you've used a textbook. You can give your child one high school credit when they have completed a high school level textbook.

If you're pulling things together yourself, whether using delight directed learning or a hodgepodge of unit studies, then give your child credit based on 120-180 hours of work. You don't have to count every hour; if they worked one hour a day on science for most of the year, it will equal enough hours for a credit. If your child does the work as a group, a credit can be awarded for the same amount of hours, for instance working four or five hours per week with their group most of the school year. Include a completion date on the transcript so colleges know when your child completed the course. Round the date to the nearest month.

Course Descriptions

Course descriptions are an important part of your child's college application package. For science, you want to write an accurate description of the class content and the resources used. It can simply be a one-paragraph description. If you need a bit of help getting started, try: "In this class, the student will study biology and demonstrate an understanding of the concepts ..."

Include a list of everything you used, including textbooks, supplements, and field trips. Also include a description of how you put together your grade. You can simply state, "1/3 tests, 1/3 quizzes, 1/3 daily work." Instead of fractions, you may choose to include percentages. It is a mistake to grade based only on tests.

All public schools incorporate more than tests in their grading systems.

Most colleges don't require documentation for sciences or excessive math and science classes at all, but some do. One college may require an emphasis on music or art instead but still wants to make sure your child meets the general science requirement. The most important thing for parents to do is research colleges where their children may apply in future. Find out each college's specific requirements.

Chapter 9

Science Tests to Take

There are many high school subject tests to choose from that will help measure science knowledge. Perhaps you have already heard about the AP Test or AP classes from your homeschool group. Maybe you have heard about required SAT Subject Tests, or wondered about CLEP tests after hearing them mentioned at a convention seminar. Which science subject test does your child need to take?

It's not necessary for parents to give tests in all subject areas, but it won't hurt your child to take a test from time to time and it may even help. Giving some tests can help children prepare for real life. Children need to take fill-in-the-bubble tests to get their beginner's permits to drive, as well as timed-tests in college classes.

College bound students, especially those destined for selective schools, should consider taking subject tests. Subject tests can be helpful as a common measurement of a student's understanding of the material.

Science subject tests are particularly helpful in providing outside documentation to reinforce the rigor of your homeschool science classes. Colleges that might otherwise be skeptical of a homeschool science class are quickly put at ease by a strong grade in a science subject test.

Most students take subject tests in their sophomore and junior year so their results are ready to present to colleges with their applications in senior year. Some students take them even earlier. In most cases, tests should be given immediately after study of the subject is completed, so the information is still fresh. In other words, have your child take the chemistry exam right after they finish their chemistry class.

Most colleges require either the SAT or the ACT test as outside documentation, but some want more in the form of subject tests. Many colleges understand these tests, and some require them for admission. Not all require SAT Subject tests. Fewer still require AP Exams. Colleges don't **require** CLEP tests, but some **accept** them, to strengthen the college application.

The ACT Test

The SAT test covers reading, writing, and math. The ACT test covers reading, writing, math, and science reasoning.

If a college requires science testing, the ACT test may satisfy them, providing outside documentation that your child understands a high school level of material. The ACT test assumes children are in the process of taking the core science courses. The test itself presents scientific information in different ways, including graphs, tables, charts, or other schematics. Your child has to figure out what they mean.

Questions may not be specific to biology or chemistry, but more about understanding the representation of data. The test gives research summaries with conflicting viewpoints with questions asking the child to analyze them. The ACT test is a high school level test, so it's not too difficult, and most kids are able to earn a reasonable score.

SAT Subject Tests

Another high school level test used to demonstrate science knowledge is the SAT Subject Test (not to be confused with the SAT test used for college admission). Subjects include biology, chemistry, and physics. These tests are one hour long, multiple-choice, and each is on a specific subject.

SAT Subject Tests are short, don't require specialized learning, and are intended to demonstrate general high school knowledge. Any textbook or curriculum will help your child study and pass the SAT Subject Test in biology, chemistry, or physics. If your child is not strong in science, or if a college requires outside documentation, an SAT Subject Test is usually the quickest, cheapest, and easiest way to demonstrate science knowledge.

Public and private high schools usually host subject tests. The SAT Subject Tests are offered multiple times a year, often at the same location as the SAT or ACT exams.

Reasons for Choosing SAT Subject Tests:

1. They are required by some colleges
2. They are required by YOUR college, as you found out during a college search
3. You are unsure what to put on the transcript, and these tests indicate knowledge of the subject

AP Tests

Another subject level test available for science (at a college or honors level) is the AP test. AP tests are offered in biology, chemistry, four branches of physics, environmental science, and computer science.

You can choose to have your child take AP classes. If your child takes an AP class, the class title on the transcript can be "AP Biology." The company that makes the AP test only allows use of the AP designation if your child takes the classes. However, your child can take the AP test without taking an AP class. In other words, you can teach "Honors Biology" at home and take the AP test. Don't name the class "AP Biology" on the transcript in this case. Instead, use "Advanced Biology" or "Honors Biology" when your child takes the AP test but not the AP class. While AP Tests assume that a student has taken rigorous AP classes approved by the College Board. Special AP classes are not required.

AP Tests are three hours long, most of them include essays, and they measure a college amount of knowledge. AP testing takes place in the spring each year.

Reasons for choosing AP Tests:

1. Confidence your child will have every test that might be required
2. Reduce cost of college by earning college credit for work done in high school
3. Success with college studies, because AP study mimics college work

CLEP Tests

CLEP tests are also an option. Like AP exams, they are at the college level. CLEP tests are available in biology, natural sciences (for an overview science class), chemistry, and psychology (which can count as a science, social studies, or social science).

CLEP tests are computer-based, multiple-choice exams offered year round that can provide college credit.

They assume students have learned naturally through reading books, visiting museums, reading the paper, and engaging in hands-on learning. These exams are often a great fit for homeschoolers because they don't assume everything was learned in a classroom setting.

Reasons for choosing CLEP

1. Earn a college degree by taking many exams that are accredited by a college
2. Reduce the cost of college by taking a few exams for college credit
3. Validate learning in specific subjects, so colleges know the sum of your child's knowledge

Honors Classes

How do you teach honors science to prepare for these tests? You can purchase an honors curriculum. Look for a textbook marked as Honors, Advanced, or AP. You can also do a Google search for public school course descriptions to see how others have taught honors science classes for ideas. You may find some great ideas for grading criteria as well.

What is an honors science class? There's no set definition, but it usually means a class at above high school level, or beyond average. Indicate an honors class with your class title, for example, "Honors Biology."

When your child takes an outside honors class with test scores, you don't have to report the test scores on the transcript unless you want to. Only put test scores on the transcript if it makes your child look smarter.

How to Decide

Choose the best test for your child. If your child is taking advanced classes and wants to attend a selective college, an AP test may be best. Independent learners with advanced knowledge might perform best on a CLEP test. If your child is working at grade level, but not taking honors classes, then perhaps

SAT Subject Tests are best. If you aren't sure what your child's level is in a subject, or if you are unschooling, then SAT Subject Tests might be helpful.

A college may require SAT Subject Tests. Some colleges require up to five or more SAT Subject Tests from all applicants (not just homeschoolers). It can help to know which tests your chosen colleges require ahead of time, and then try to exceed their expectations for college admission and scholarship success. You can meet or exceed their expectations by having your child take tests that make them look most desirable. Do an online search for the names of your college choices plus "admission requirements." Remember that college policies change over time, so contact the college directly, before senior year, to find out any additional, updated information.

Of course, the difficulty is knowing which colleges your child may want to attend. If you can't determine this in advance, let me give you a one-size-fits-most suggestion. Plan to have your child take five SAT Subject Tests, one during sophomore year, and two each during junior year and senior year. This is usually the number required by colleges that want to see subject tests.

Whichever test you choose, make sure your child takes the test soon after completing the subject so they know the material.

Once subject tests are done, you have the option of including test scores on your homeschool transcript. If the scores make your child look smarter (good scores), then include them on the transcript. If the scores do not make your child look smarter (bad scores), then leave them off the transcript.

While you do need to meet college admission requirements, if these tests aren't right for your child, there are other ways to earn outside documentation. Dual enrollment, letters of recommendation, comprehensive homeschool records, excellent application essays, and a work resume can also increase your child's chances of earning college admission and scholarships. Learn more about outside documentation by reading my article at: www.thehomescholar.com/ outsidedocumentation.php.

Know your child and trust yourself. As always, do what's best for your child.

Helpful Tips

Register for each test months in advance so you don't miss the deadline, but don't let your student take a test unprepared. Have your child take a sample test at home, to make sure they know the material. Then help them study for the test using study guides at home, filling in any small gaps in the information. Sit your child down to take a full-length, timed sample test, to be sure the student can succeed with the timing and the format of the test. Then have them take the real test at a testing location.

The bottom line is, never have your child take a test if you believe they will not pass. It can hurt your child's future testing ability, and cause problems with their self-perception. Pre-test at home to make sure your child is comfortable with the material and the test format. Only have them take a real test once you are confident they can pass it. If you aren't certain your child will earn an acceptable score, don't have scores sent to colleges until after you have seen the results.

Remember, it's unusual for a child to go to college classes or take a college test without feeling some stress. A bit of stress can be helpful, so children can learn to deal with stressful test situations. On the other hand, you don't want to build anxiety up in your child needlessly until they develop a phobia of tests. You don't want to ask them to take a test they aren't comfortable with.

Once you have decided on which tests you want your child to take, keep track of test dates. Each year, add important dates to your calendar or planner, including registration deadlines, the date of each test, and dates you will receive results. Include the location and test code you will need on test day.

These test codes are called CEEB codes, which are standardized ID numbers assigned to high schools, colleges, and universities by the Educational Testing Service (ETS). They are mostly used for college entrance exams such as the SAT and ACT, but are also used by NCAA sports, sports teams, and academic teams. Many universities have opted to use CEEB codes on their applications. To avoid mistakes, most applications do not allow manual entry of the codes during online registration. Instead, they rely on a school code search by state, which can be confusing.

Here are the codes you will need for subject tests:

- ACT Homeschool Code: 969999
- SAT Subject Test Homeschool Code: 970-000.
- AP Test Homeschool Code: provided by test coordinator. (You may want to call the test administrator in advance and tell them your homeschooled student is coming in for testing, so they have the code available.)

Here is the good news – the test proctors will know the homeschool code! Don't panic if you forget to write it down, because someone in charge can tell you what it is, or will know how to find the information. Even so, it can put your mind at ease to keep these homeschool codes handy.

When you use the homeschool code, the testing company will contact you directly with test results, instead of sending it to the local high school and rely on them to give you the test results. You will often receive the scores weeks sooner when you use the homeschool code. Send the test results to each college during senior year, if you haven't before then.

There are four steps for test preparation. First, your child has to learn the subject, using curriculum and resources that match their learning style. While the subject is still fresh in their mind, pick up a study guide for the test to prepare your child for the exact questions they will encounter. Next, you need to identify the information they haven't learned yet - topics that might be on the test but weren't covered in the curriculum. Take the time to fill any gaps. Finally, have your child take sample tests repeatedly, to practice timing, speed, filling in bubbles, and writing essays. This will help them earn the maximum scores possible. If sample test scores aren't very good, consider other tests or options. There are many things you can do to improve your child's test score beyond test preparation. Sleep, nutrition, and hydration are remarkably important.

Testing Resources

Choosing a study guide and resources can be a challenge. Read online reviews first, because study guides change frequently. The resources below will help you decide on the right test, check out the format, and locate independent study guides you can use at home.

SAT Subject Tests

Research SAT Subject Tests: sat.collegeboard.org/about-tests/sat-subject-tests

Take Sample SAT Subject Tests using The Official Study Guide for All SAT Subject Tests by The College Board: www.amazon.com/gp/product/ 0874477565

Choose Study Guides for SAT Subject Tests (I prefer Princeton Review Books): www.amazon.com/gp/product/0307945 561

AP Tests

Research AP Subject Tests: apstudent.collegeboard.org/home

Take Sample AP Subject Tests: apstudent.collegeboard.org/ takingtheexam/preparing-for-exams

Choose Study Guides for AP Subject Tests (I prefer Princeton Review Books): www.amazon.com/Cracking-Chemistry-Edition-College-Preparation/dp/ 0804126143

CLEP Exams

Research CLEP Exams: clep.collegeboard.org/started

Take Sample CLEP Exams with CLEP Official Study Guide by The College Board: www.amazon.com/gp/product/ 1457304619

Choose Study Guides for CLEP Exams (I prefer CLEP Study Guides by REA): http://www.amazon.com/gp/product/ 0738611026

If you need additional help, look to the test prep companies specifically geared to the test you need, such as Kaplan (www.kaptest.com) and The Princeton Review (www. princetonreview.com). You can also hire a tutor. While a general tutor may be helpful for general subjects and test taking strategies, specific tests may require targeted preparation. Look for tutors and classes with specific expertise.

Afterword

Who is Lee Binz and What Can She Do for Me?

Number one best-selling homeschool author, Lee Binz is The HomeScholar. Her mission is "helping parents homeschool high school." Lee and her husband Matt homeschooled their two boys, Kevin and Alex, from elementary through high school.

Upon graduation, both boys received four-year, full tuition scholarships from their first choice university. This enables Lee to pursue her dream job - helping parents homeschool their children through high school.

On The HomeScholar website, you will find great products for creating homeschool transcripts and comprehensive records to help you amaze and impress colleges.

Find out why Andrew Pudewa, Founder of the Institute for Excellence in Writing says, "Lee Binz knows how to navigate this often confusing and frustrating labyrinth better than anyone."

You can find Lee online at:

www.TheHomeScholar.com

If this book has been helpful, could you please take a minute to write us a quick review on Amazon?

Thank you!

Testimonials

Calming and Practical Advice

"Our daughter had chronic Lyme Disease. I was stressed wondering how we were going to get her through High School. Then I found you! With your ebooks, emails and blog I was able to create a high school centered on her interests and be creative with how she learned each subject. Your clear method for keeping course work and making transcripts was so easy that I was even able to help friends when they struggled. I couldn't have done it without you Lee!

I feel like I know you and if I ever see you I will definitely give you a hug because you helped me to see that homeschooling high school doesn't have to be hard, overwhelming or impossible."

~ Tricia

Scholarships Worth 93% of College Costs!

Dear Lee,

"I have been so blessed by your newsletters, website, and the Total Transcript Solution. Last October, my daughter was accepted and awarded the highest academic scholarship from all four of the private Christian colleges she applied to. Two of those universities invited her to compete for "up to full-tuition scholarships," and in early April, she was awarded the Presidential Honors Scholarship at the University for her well-written essay. She was also awarded a vocal/music scholarship after I encouraged her to audition even though she had an insignificant amount of vocal training! All combined, Michaela was awarded 93% of her tuition for four years. Room, board, and books are virtually her only responsibility.

Know that I recently met with the Director of the Honors Program at the University who identified with interest, an unusual activity Michaela completed during high school that was listed on her TTS transcript. The Total Transcript Solution made it easier for the university to conclude that Michaela's unique homeschooling experiences would be a welcome addition to the University community!

Thank you for your sound advice on starting a high school folder. The best thing I ever did was start Michaela's transcripts when she started doing high school work–and that was in 8th grade. And every time we did something, a college class or a field trip, a conference, or a missions project, anything... I printed it off the internet, dated it, and put it in a folder. That little nugget of advice from you has SAVED me. One of the essay scholarship questions on the application was, "What kinds of extra-curricular cultural activities have you done?" Fortunately, I found ticket stubs in Michaela's folder from a Latin museum and a Latino Film Festival we forgot she attended two years earlier for her extra-credit Spanish coursework at the community college. Every parent should have a folder, whether they are homeschooling or not!

Thank you for your dedication and service to the homeschooling community. Your recommendations and resources have empowered me to take control of my children's high school education. I know that we will complete high school with absolute success

Hopefully this will give more parents hope to keep their children out of the public school system. We need to keep sending a message that it can be done!"

~ Kathleen

For more information about my
Total Transcript Solution, go to:

www.TheHomeScholar.com/
TotalTranscriptSolution.php

Also From
The HomeScholar...

- The HomeScholar Guide to College Admission and Scholarships: Homeschool Secrets to Getting Ready, Getting In and Getting Paid (Book and Kindle Book)
- Setting the Records Straight - How to Craft Homeschool Transcripts and Course Descriptions for College Admission and Scholarships (Book and Kindle Book)
- Total Transcript Solution (Online Training, Tools and Templates)
- Comprehensive Record Solution (Online Training, Tools and Templates)

- Gold Care Club (Comprehensive Online Support and Training)
- Preparing to Homeschool High School (DVD)
- Finding a College (DVD)
- The Easy Truth About Homeschool Transcripts (Kindle Book)
- Parent Training A la Carte (Online Training)
- Homeschool "Convention at Home" Kit (Book, DVDs and Audios)

The HomeScholar "Coffee Break Books" Released or Coming Soon on Kindle and Paperback:

- Delight Directed Learning: Guiding Your Homeschooler Toward Passionate Learning
- Creating Transcripts for Your Unique Child: Help Your Homeschool Graduate Stand Out from the Crowd
- Beyond Academics: Preparation for College and for Life
- Planning High School Courses: Charting the Course Toward High School Graduation
- Graduate Your Homeschooler in Style: Make Your Homeschool Graduation Memorable

- Keys to High School Success: Get Your Homeschool High School Started Right!
- Getting the Most Out of Your Homeschool This Summer: Learning just for the Fun of it!
- Finding a College: A Homeschooler's Guide to Finding a Perfect Fit
- College Scholarships for High School Credit: Learn and Earn With This Two-for-One Strategy!
- College Admission Policies Demystified: Understanding Homeschool Requirements for Getting In
- A Higher Calling: Homeschooling High School for Harried Husbands (by Matt Binz, Mr. HomeScholar)
- Gifted Education Strategies for Every Child: Homeschool Secrets for Success
- College Application Essays: A Primer for Parents
- Creating Homeschool Balance: Find Harmony Between Type A and Type Zzz...
- Homeschooling the Holidays: Sanity Saving Strategies and Gift Giving Ideas
- Your Goals this Year: A Year by Year Guide to Homeschooling High School

- Making the Grades: A Grouch-Free Guide to Homeschool Grading
- High School Testing: Knowledge That Saves Money
- Getting the BIG Scholarships: Learn Expert Secrets for Winning College Cash!
- Easy English for Simple Homeschooling: How to Teach, Assess and Document High School English
- Scheduling - The Secret to Homeschool Sanity: Plan You Way Back to Mental Health
- Junior Year is the Key to High School Success: How to Unlock the Gate to Graduation and Beyond
- Upper Echelon Education: How to Gain Admission to Elite Universities
- How to Homeschool College: Save Time, Reduce Stress and Eliminate Debt
- Homeschool Curriculum That's Effective and Fun: Avoid the Crummy Curriculum Hall of Shame!
- Comprehensive Homeschool Records: Put Your Best Foot Forward to Win College Admission and Scholarships
- Options After High School: Steps to Success for College or Career

- How to Homeschool 9th and 10th Grade: Simple Steps for Starting Strong!
- Senior Year Step-by-Step: Simple Instructions for Busy Homeschool Parents
- High School Math The Easy Way: Simple Strategies for Homeschool Parents In Over Their Heads
- How to Homeschool Independently: Do-it-Yourself Secrets to Rekindle the Love of Learning
- Homeschooling Middle School with Powerful Purpose: How to Successfully Navigate 6th through 8th Grade

Would you like to be notified when we offer one of our *Coffee Break Books* for FREE during our Kindle promotion days? If so, leave your name and email at the link below and we will send you a reminder.

http://www.TheHomeScholar.com/freekindlebook.php

Visit my Amazon Author Page!

amazon.com/author/leebinz

64713430R00064

Made in the USA
Lexington, KY
17 June 2017